599
MCD

McDearmon, Kay

The walrus: giant of
the Arctic ice

DATE		
OCT 27, 77		
JAN 2 0 1978		
MAR 3 1978		
MAR 1 6 1979		
NOV 3 0 1979		
MAR 1 7 1980		
MAR 2 1 1980		
NOV 5		

THE WALRUS:
Giant of the Arctic Ice

THE WALRUS:
Giant of the Arctic Ice

Kay McDearmon

Illustrated with photographs

DODD, MEAD & COMPANY · NEW YORK

PICTURE CREDITS

John J. Burns, Alaska Department of Fish and Game, pages 2, 13, 19, 21, 28; Marineland of the Pacific Photographs, by Bob Noble, pages 29, 33, 34; Picture Collection, California Academy of Sciences, pages 25, 42; San Diego Zoo Photographs, pages 10, 14, 16, 22, 26, 39; U.S. Department of Commerce, National Marine Fisheries Service, pages 23, 44; U.S. Fish and Wildlife Service, page 17; University of Alaska Archives, Lomen Family Collection, page 36.

To Jennifer

INTRODUCTORY NOTE

Walruses live mainly in the cold Arctic seas that en-circle the globe. They rarely stray far from the southern edge of the polar pack ice.

Scientists recognize two varieties or subspecies of walrus. One is the Pacific walrus (*Odobenus rosmarus divergens*) that inhabits the icy waters off northwest Alaska and northeast Siberia. The other variety is the Atlantic walrus (*Odobenus rosmarus rosmarus*). It is scattered in the eastern Arctic seas from northern Can-ada to Greenland, and north of Norway.

The two kinds of walruses look very much alike, but the Pacific walrus is larger than his Atlantic cousin. Some Pacific bulls weigh 4000 pounds. The biggest Atlantic bulls are about 1000 pounds lighter.

The nostrils of the Pacific walrus are higher on his head, and his whiskers are shorter. Tusks differ, too. A Pacific walrus' tusks may be as long as thirty inches. The tusks of an Atlantic walrus are shorter, and usually straighter and slimmer.

Wherever they live, walruses have similar habits, but they differ widely in the distances they migrate. The Pacific walrus may travel 2000 miles, while the seasonal trips of the Atlantic walrus may total less than 100 miles.

At present there are about 125,000 walruses in the world. About 75 per cent of these are Pacific walruses. Years ago many more of both kinds lived in the polar seas. However, hunters vastly reduced their numbers.

As a result, the Atlantic walrus is still on the endangered species list. Now the Pacific walrus, the subject of this book, is slowly recovering. The latest laws are intended to insure the continued existence of this fascinating sea mammal.

THE WALRUS:
Giant of the Arctic Ice

ONE spring day while on their yearly journey north, a mother walrus and her calf scrambled off their ice floe to swim in the cold, black waters of the Bering Sea between Alaska and Russia.

For a while they swam alongside each other. Then, feeling adventurous, the calf swam off by himself. Soon, even though he rolled his red, bulging eyes in all directions, he couldn't see his mother.

So the frightened calf began to bark. His mother heard him, splashed through the sea to him, and led him back to the herd on the ice floe.

She was a huge, clumsy-looking creature. Her pudgy body was a mass of wrinkles and folds. Long whiskers drooped over her mouth, and two long tusks protruded from underneath her upper lip. And she looked about with soulful eyes.

Now, full-grown, she was nine feet long, and weighed a ton. She used her four flippers to shuffle along on ice floes and sometimes on land, and to propel herself through the water.

As a mammal, she was a warm-blooded animal that breathed air and nursed her young. She was a member of a group of sea animals called Pinnipedia, meaning fin-footed. Seals, sea lions, and sea elephants also belong to this group.

Although the walrus is now a sea mammal, scientists believe that long ago walruses had legs and lived on land. Over a period of millions of years their four legs gradually evolved into webbed flippers, and they adapted to a life in and near the water.

Like all walruses, the mother spent much time traveling and resting on floating islands of ice called floes. Her calf had been born on the ice while the herds were returning from their winter homes to the Arctic the previous spring. At birth he weighed a hefty one hun-

dred pounds. Now, a year later, he was already the size of a full-grown lion.

The calf never saw his father. The male and female had remained together for only a short while during

the mating season. Afterward, the father returned to his herd, composed entirely of males, and never visited the mother again.

From the calf's birth, his mother furnished all his needs. She nursed him while lying on the ice or in the water. From drinking her rich milk, he gradually developed a layer of blubber under his hide to help keep him warm. His hair, no longer needed for warmth, thinned out and changed from silver to brown.

From the beginning, the mother walrus showered her calf with affection. Tucking him between her flippers, she cuddled him. She gently stroked his hair, and she often played with him on the edge of their ice floe.

Sometimes she tossed him like a ball from flipper to flipper. Once she accidentally dropped him into the sea. She plunged into the water after him, and quickly rescued him.

The young walrus was not really helpless in the water. He could paddle around on the surface and make short dives a few days after his birth, but he would bawl when his mother shoved him into the sea. With-

15

in a few months he could swim and dive well. After that, he seemed to enjoy the water.

But for some time his mother continued to carry him with her wherever she went. On the surface he rode on her back. When she dived for food, she clasped him to her breast, and he held on tight with his flippers.

If she were to leave him on the ice while she went
food-hunting, a hungry polar bear might grab him for
his supper. Or a killer whale might tip the ice, capturing the calf when he fell into the sea.

During the frigid nights he slept on top of his mother's warm body, or snuggled up alongside it. To protect her baby from the herd, she selected a resting place a little apart from the other mothers. This way the massive body of a full-grown walrus couldn't smother him.

When danger threatened, her first concern was for her calf. One day a low-flying airplane roared over the herd, alarming her. She shoved her young one off the ice before diving into the sea herself.

She rarely took her eyes off her baby during his first year. But shortly before beginning their migration this spring, she became friendly with a giant bull, weighing nearly two tons, with tusks thirty inches long. He appeared while she was swimming, and they mated before parting.

Now, she and her year-old calf were part of a large nursery herd traveling back to the Arctic on their yearly spring journey. Many such groups were also cruising north, each on its own ice floe. Large herds of males, or bulls, drifted along on other floes. Riding on still

others were females without babies. And now and then a family group drifted along on a single floe.

Altogether, about 90,000 Pacific walruses were migrating north that year. They were only part of a vast, scattered parade. Thousands of birds, seals, and whales were also traveling through the Bering Strait.

But while the herds drifted along on ice floes—some larger than a baseball field—the walruses all faced dangers.

On stormy days fierce gales tossed the smaller floes around. Then the nursery herd remained awake and watchful, ready to scramble back from the edge, or dive into the water. Otherwise, if another floe crashed into theirs, some of them might be crushed.

One day a walrus, returning from a dive to the ocean floor, found that her ice floe had moved quite a distance. She had to race to catch it. Though she was a good swimmer, she couldn't maintain her top speed for long. Luckily, she reached the drifting floe before she became exhausted.

Altogether on their journey back to the Arctic from

their winter homes far to the south, the walruses might travel as much as one thousand miles. When their ice floes weren't moving in the right direction, they would dive into the sea and swim for a while, then catch floes going their way.

When the mother walrus wanted to climb upon a floe, she, like other adult walruses, used her powerful ivory tusks to dig into the ice. Then she pulled herself to the edge, grasped it with her foreflippers, and pushed herself onto the surface. The walruses' family name is Odobenidae, or "tooth-walkers," which comes from their habit of using their tusks to help them "walk."

21

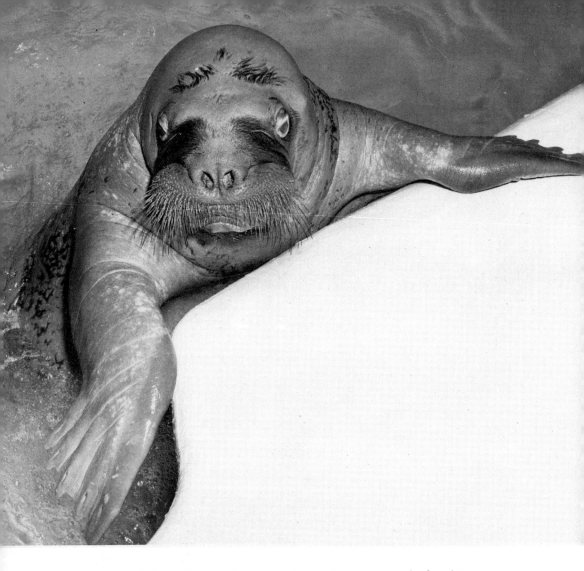

The calf's tusks weren't yet long enough for him to use them in this fashion, but he could leap out of the water onto an ice floe. He and other walruses slithered across the ice without slipping because the palms of their foreflippers and the soles of their hind flippers were rough and hard.

In no rush to reach the Arctic, sometimes the walruses climbed out of the water to rest after a swim. When

only rocky shores were close, the adult walruses waited for the surf to lift them gradually, and then they climbed on shore, using their long, gleaming white tusks. By doing this, the walruses avoided damaging their tusks by scraping them against the rocks.

After a pleasant rest, the walruses resumed their journey. Each herd traveled at its own speed. As they funneled through Bering Strait, some turned toward Russia. Others, including the nursery herd, continued along the Alaskan coast to Barrow. It was mid-summer before all the herds ended their journey in the Arctic Ocean.

The mighty polar bear was then traveling near the northern tip of Alaska in search of food. It was unlikely that he would attack the full-grown mother walrus. In the water, the walrus was faster, and a well-placed thrust from her tusks could kill him. On land it was useless for a white bear to sneak up on her unless she was too far away from the water to be able to escape into it.

But one time a polar bear, standing upon a high cliff, threw a large block of ice at a walrus resting below, and hit him.

However, the polar bear usually saved his efforts almost entirely for capturing calves. He sometimes cruised in the sea, with only his black nose appearing above the surface. Then, just as he reached an ice floe, he would seize a walrus calf near the edge, and pull it into the water for his supper.

One day a crafty polar bear hid behind a snowbank on the mother's floe. When she and her calf started to dive into the sea, the big bear emerged from his hiding place, and made a quick grab for the calf. Luckily, this time the bear caught only the calf's slippery hind flippers, and the baby escaped.

Actually, most of the walruses' summer days were peaceful and quiet. On sunny days (and there are sunny days even in the Arctic) the herd often lay on the ice for hours. When the walrus mother or any of the others became uncomfortably warm, they fanned themselves with their foreflippers.

Once the mother rested so long in one spot that the ice melted under her, and she found herself almost submerged in a pool of water.

As they lay on the ice, the members of the nursery herd were bothered by sea lice and other insect-like creatures. They wandered among the folds of the walruses' baggy, leathery skin. They even meandered around the calves' nostrils and necks.

At times seabirds landed on the animals, and pecked

at the marine creatures. This helped some, but to try to banish more of them, the walruses often scratched them with their foreflippers.

Since it was summer, walruses were shedding their old hair, and growing new coats. Herds of bellowing bulls stretched out on beaches or ice floes, pillowed on each other, and slept for about two weeks until their new, sparse, reddish-brown hair appeared.

Bulls often fasted during this moulting period, but the mothers, needing food to nurse their calves, continued eating.

The walruses dived to the nearly dark sea floor for
their food. They usually surfaced after about four minutes, but they could remain submerged for as long as
ten minutes. They could do this because walruses store
much more oxygen in their blood cells than land mammals do.

The heart of a walrus normally beats 150 times a minute—about twice as fast as a human being's—but when the walrus dives, it slows down to only about ten beats. This reduces the use of oxygen, and enables the walrus to hold his breath longer.

The mother walrus preferred to eat clams, mussels, and snails, but sometimes she also dined on sea cucumbers, sea urchins, worms, and many other bottom-dwelling animals. On occasion, she ate fish and consumed roots of marine plants.

Most of the sea creatures that the herd ate lay close to the surface of the muddy bottom, and the walruses rooted around for them. To help locate them, they felt about with their stiff, sensitive whiskers. About four hundred of these whiskers, each with their own blood vessels and nerves, extended from the fleshy pads on their upper lips. Walruses' whiskers are the longest at the corners of their mouths. The center ones gradually wear down as they probe for food on the sea floor.

When the mother walrus captured the larger clams

and snails, she would suck out the soft parts, then drop the shell. When she tackled the smaller clams and mussels, she broke the shells with her lips or mouth, or both, then discarded them before swallowing the parts she preferred. As crocodiles do, she sometimes swallowed pebbles. Some scientists believe these pebbles help grind up food or bits of shell that the walruses might accidentally swallow.

Ordinarily, the walruses' diet does not include other mammals. But when a whale carcass drifts onto the beach where a herd of bulls is resting, the bulls may sample it.

Walruses that eat seals are usually rejected by their fellows. One day when a strong wind split the nursery herd's floe, separating one of the mothers from her calf, an Eskimo hunter killed the mother.

For three days the calf cried for her and, deprived of her milk, he became hungrier and hungrier. Finally, the starving orphan caught a few seals and ate them. Shortly after, he located the herd, but it drove him away

31

because of his different smell. He was forced to become a wanderer, or rogue.

Fortunately, such unhappy incidents were rare. Most days the nursery herd fared well, and enjoyed long periods of rest. The walruses dozed while ashore, on ice floes, or in openings in the ice.

In icy waters, walruses usually sleep floating on their backs or bellies. Sometimes they sleep under breathing holes in the ice, rising between short naps to grab the edge of the ice with their tusks, breathe, and go back to sleep.

A sac under the throat of an adult walrus fills with air and helps to hold his nose out of the water. This enables the walrus to sleep even in an upright position in the sea.

One day the mother walrus slumbered that way long enough for a layer of ice to develop around her. The ice crackled as she forced her way out of it.

The males particularly disliked being disturbed when they slept on the ice. If a neighbor poked one, he would awaken, bellow, and slap the nearest walrus with his

flippers. The slapped animal would roar, and in turn, hit a neighbor. Before long, the whole herd of bulls would be awake, and all bellowing. The walrus is so noisy at times, that he has been called "the loudest voice in the Arctic." Moments later, however, they would all be napping again.

While the walruses liked to sleep, especially when they were huddled together, they also enjoyed playing. They rode the cresting waves up and down, and turned somersaults in the water.

The calves in the nursery herd were more active than their mothers. They dived into the water over and over, chased each other, and nipped at each other's flippers. When they tired of such games, they leaped from the sea onto ice floes, and tumbled back into the water again.

With nostrils located high on their heads, the walruses could breathe in the water when only a tiny part of their body was above the surface. But if they swam too far below the ice, or the ice suddenly froze above them, they might not have had time to reach an opening in the ice.

Adult walruses in the various herds solved this by opening breathing holes. Swimming below the ice, they would strike the ice again and again with their heavy heads. If this didn't shatter the ice, they would float on their backs, and tap the ice with their strong tusks until they opened a circle in it. They then pushed their heads

35

through the holes. Sometimes walruses teamed together to open breathing holes.

But as the short Arctic summer ended, the ice became thicker. When it was over four inches thick, the walruses couldn't keep their breathing holes open, and sought thinner ice farther south.

So, in the fall they started migrating to warmer waters again. One by one, huge herds, pods of forty or so walruses, and a few family groups left the Arctic on their floating ice. They traveled in a more leisurely fashion now than they did in the spring. Occasionally

a herd of bulls climbed onto an island beach and rested there for a week at a time.

But however slowly they moved, they all drifted through the Bering Strait before it froze over, and kept traveling to their favorite winter homes in the Bering Sea.

Some of the herds continued until they reached the area of the Walrus Islands off the southern coast of Alaska. The nursery herd didn't journey quite so far.

The walruses chose their seasonal homes with great care. They selected areas where clams were plentiful enough to satisfy their enormous appetites. Since walruses dive to the sea floor for their food, and they cannot dive more than about 250 feet, they also chose fairly shallow water. Most of them also settled near an ice floe, so they could rest on it when they left the water.

When there were no floes close by, the walruses climbed on rocky shores or beaches. When the bulls scrambled ashore, they would compete for choice locations. One time a young bull dragged himself along an island beach flipper by flipper, trying to force his way through the herd. He jabbed his tusks at the animals in his way. Some struck back, making him pay for his progress.

But when the herd saw the largest bulls coming, they moved and made a path for them, and the bigger males had no need to strike any of their fellows.

One day the mother walrus and her calf, along with the rest of the nursery herd, all tried to crowd together on a small ice floe. Before long it started to sink, finally capsizing and tumbling them all into the water.

As the mother walrus looked around anxiously for her baby, she saw him swimming toward her. When they met, she led him to another floe close by.

One day that winter she almost lost her calf. He was shuffling along on the ice when he fell into a crevasse hidden by snow.

His mother saw him fall, but when she peered into the opening, she saw that the split in the ice was too deep and narrow to allow her to rescue him. Instead, using her tusks, she chopped away at the ice until she widened the opening. Her calf was then able to pull himself out.

Winter brought new dangers to the nursery herd. A few Eskimos were hunting with dog teams on the ice in the area. When the dogs found fresh breathing holes, the hunters patiently waited for a walrus to poke up his head for air. When it did, they flung sharp-pointed harpoons into the unlucky animal.

Most danger from hunters came after the ice started to break up in the spring. One Eskimo village stationed a man high atop a cliff. Looking through field glasses, he scanned the area. Meanwhile, veteran hunters were ready to grab their rifles and jump into their skin boats, some now equipped with motors. Fortunately, that day the Eskimo did not see the nursery herd.

When the hunters sighted walruses and fired at them from their boats, they avoided getting too close to the animals. When provoked, a herd of usually peaceful walruses could be fierce foes.

Sometimes the walruses grabbed the hunter's paddles, and broke them in two. Sometimes they ripped open the bottom of their boats with their tusks. Or they used their tusks to overturn boats, and then attacked the hunters they had dumped into the sea. And if any walrus was wounded, their fellows closed in to attack the hunter.

To try to discourage the sea mammals from approaching their boats, some Eskimos painted the bottoms red, a color they believed frightened the walrus.

The Alaskan Eskimos have had a real need to capture walrus. Until recently, the mammals supplied almost all their needs.

The Eskimos used the skin to cover their homes and boats, and for making rope. From the bones and tusks they fashioned hunting tools. They converted the blubber to fuel, and stored the meat in ice caves and shared it with their hunting dogs. They made window covers from the intestines, and even ate the undigested clams they found in the stomachs of the walruses.

Now the Eskimos no longer live in skin-covered homes. Most of them use fuel oil, and they have metal weapons. But even today, some villages couldn't exist without the walrus.

With the arrival of spring, the time for the walruses to migrate to the Arctic was approaching once more.

Another enemy appeared in the Bering Sea that season. He was the killer whale, the walruses' most fearsome natural enemy.

The killer whale can rip a walrus to pieces with his sharp teeth. But on occasion the walrus emerges the victor. One day, a bull trapped alone in the water stabbed a whale with his tusks, and killed him. The walrus was close enough to his floe to scramble back before the pack of forty whales caught up with him.

Another day a herd of bulls was swimming in the sea when they heard the beat of the killer whales' flukes. The walrus herd thrashed through the surf, and climbed onto the nearby beach. There the panic-stricken beasts piled up on top of each other. In their dash for safety from the pack of killer whales, several walruses were smothered.

The nursery herd was especially watchful, as walrus calves are a favorite prey of the whales. A time or two they seized a calf resting on the edge of an ice floe. Once a whale dived directly below a calf on the ice, hit the floe a mighty blow, and split the ice. Then the whale had only to open his cavernous mouth to insure himself of a meal.

One time, their anger aroused by the loss of a calf, some cows plunged into the sea in pursuit of a killer whale. He swam faster than they, and escaped.

But no killer whales came near the nursery herd, so the mother and her calf swam, dived, ate, played, and rested undisturbed.

Every day her calf was becoming bigger and stronger. His tusks were getting longer, and he was better able to defend himself. He was almost two years old now, and he was learning to secure most of his own food from the sea floor. He was becoming a young bull.

One day, knowing that her calf no longer needed her, his mother dived into the sea and swam off by herself. She headed for another ice floe, and joined a herd of cows resting there. She would have another calf later this spring during her trip north.

When his mother didn't return, the calf hardly hesitated. He calmly dived into the sea, and swam from floe to floe, until he located a herd of bulls. Then he dug his tusks into the ice, pulled himself up onto the floe, and joined them. He was now on his own.

ABOUT THE AUTHOR

Kay McDearmon was born in San Francisco and received her B.A. degree from the University of California at Berkeley. Before devoting her time to writing, she was a high school teacher and social service worker.

In addition to her present book on the walrus, she is the author of A DAY IN THE LIFE OF A SEA OTTER, and numerous newspaper and magazine articles.

Kay McDearmon lives with her husband, a professor of Speech Pathology, in Turlock, California, where leisure time activities include bicycling, swimming, reading, and music.